Wedding Album
for manuals

EDITED & ARRANGED BY

C. H. TREVOR

Order No: NOV262750

NOVELLO

EDITORIAL NOTE

Although the pieces in this book have suggestions for registration on an organ of two (and sometimes three) manuals, they can be played effectively on a one-manual instrument with appropriate stops. The pedals can be used at the player's discretion. When the dynamics only are given, the choice of registration is left to the player.

As stops with the same names do not always produce the same effect on different organs, other registrations should be used if those suggested are not effective or suitable on any particular instrument. The directions for registration in brackets may be used or not at the player's discretion.

If the organ is an unenclosed one-manual, the dynamics should be ignored except where it is possible to change the registration without interrupting the flow of the music.

Most of the pieces in this book are suitable for use on other occasions.

Certain sections and repeats may be omitted if a piece is found to be too long for the required time.

C.H.T.

CONTENTS

			Page
Bridal Chorus		WAGNER	3
St. Anthony Chorale	attributed to	HAYDN	4
Wedding March		MENDELSSOHN	5
Suite from the 'Water Music'		HANDEL	9
Minuet		BEETHOVEN	17
Entr'acte		SCHUBERT	18
Processional		MENDELSSOHN	19
Interlude		MUFFAT	19
Air (from Suite No. 3)		J. S. BACH	20
Minuet		J. S. BACH	21
Trumpet Voluntary		CLARKE	22
Voluntary in G (Op. 6, No. 7)		STANLEY	24
Gavotte		ARNE	28
Minuet		PURCELL	30
Rigadon		PURCELL	30
Largo		HANDEL	31
Musette		HANDEL	32

BRIDAL CHORUS

Gt. 8. 4.
Sw. 8. 4. 2. } or Diapason 8.
Sw. to Gt.

Wagner
(1813—1883)

Con moto moderato
Sw.
Gt.
Sw.
Gt.
Sw.
Gt.
Sw.
rall.

4

ST. ANTHONY CHORALE

Gt. 8. 4.
Sw. 8. 4. box closed.
Sw. to Gt.

Attributed to Haydn
(1732—1809)

This piece can be used as a Processional with or without repeats.

WEDDING MARCH

Mendelssohn
(1809—1847)

6

The shakes can be omitted.

SUITE FROM THE "WATER MUSIC"

Handel
(1685—1759)

1. Introduction

This piece can be used as a Processional with or without repeats.

2. Minuet

Gt. (or Ch.) Flute(s) 8. (4.)
Sw. Diapason 8.

3. Air

4. Siciliana

If preferred, this piece can be played on the Swell throughout.

5. Hornpipe

6. Aria

Gt. (or Ch.) } Diapason 8. (or Flutes 8. 4.)
Sw.

repeat on Sw.

Gt. (or Ch.)

2nd time rall.

repeat on Sw.

7. Bourrée

Sw. (or Ch.) light 8. 2. (or 8. 4.)

8. Finale

The Finale can be used as a Processional with or without repeats.

MINUET

Gt. (or Ch.) Flute(s) 8. (4.)
Sw. soft 8.

Beethoven
(1770 — 1827)

ENTR'ACTE

Sw. Diapason 8.

Schubert
(1797—1828)

PROCESSIONAL
(from "Hymn of Praise")

Mendelssohn
(1809—1847)

INTERLUDE

Gottlieb Muffat
(1690—1770)

Diapason 8. (or Flutes 8. 4.)

TWO PIECES

No. 1. Air
(from "Suite No. 3")

J. S. Bach
(1685—1750)

This piece can be played on Swell soft 8ft., the box being (half) open for each section and repeated with the box (nearly) closed. Alternatively, each section can be played on soft Choir (or Great) 8ft. and repeated on softer Swell 8ft.

No. 2. Minuet

Gt. (or Ch.) Solo stop 8.
Sw. soft 8. (4.)

Allegretto

TRUMPET VOLUNTARY

I Trumpet 8. [or Diapason(s) 8. (4.)]
II 8. 4. (2.)

Jeremiah Clarke
(1659—1707)

Alternative registration for a one-manual organ: Diapasons 8. 4. (2.)

VOLUNTARY IN G
(Op. 6. No. 7)

Gt. Diapasons 8. 4. (2.)
Sw. Diapasons 8. 4. 2. (Mixture.) box open.
Sw. to Gt.

John Stanley
(1713—1786)

The composer's registration: Full Organ i.e. the full organ of his time.
The *Largo* can be used as a Processional.

E. 2750

GAVOTTE

Gt. Flute(s) 8. (4.)
Sw. 8. (Flute 4.)

Thomas Arne
(1710—1778)

TWO PIECES

No. 1. Minuet

Gt. Flute 8.
Sw. soft 8.

Henry Purcell
(1659—1695)

No. 2. Rigadon

light 8. 2. (or 8. 4.)

TWO PIECES

No. 1. Largo

Gt.
Sw.} Diapason 8.
(Sw. to Gt.)

Handel
(1685—1759)

No. 2. Musette

Andante con moto (♩ = about 104)

This piece can be played on Swell soft 8ft., the box being (half) open for each section and repeated with the box (nearly) closed.